IMAGES
of America

CHANNAHON
AND MINOOKA

IMAGES
of America

CHANNAHON
AND MINOOKA

Dawn Aulet

ARCADIA
PUBLISHING

Published by Arcadia Publishing
Charleston, South Carolina

Library of Congress Control Number: 2013930394

For all general information, please contact Arcadia Publishing:
Telephone 843-853-2070
Fax 843-853-0044
E-mail sales@arcadiapublishing.com
For customer service and orders:
Toll-Free 1-888-313-2665

Visit us on the Internet at www.arcadiapublishing.com

For Joseph Aulet and Nathaniel Aulet, may you always realize that history is the place you begin, where you design your dreams and plot your course to be whatever your hearts desire.

CONTENTS

ACKNOWLEDGMENTS

Without the expertise of Michele Houchens and the technological savvy of David Belden, this book would not have been possible. Houchens is the local history librarian at Three Rivers Library, Minooka Branch, and is a one-person history book on the towns of Minooka and Channahon. Not only does she organize and run the local history museum, which is located in the basement of the Minooka Branch, but she also is part of a multi-generation Minooka family. She can tell you not only the building pictured in a historic photograph, but also often the family story to go with it.

David Belden, himself an Arcadia author who penned *Illinois & Michigan Canal*, among other books, took an extra step and uploaded all of the library's images onto disk. This streamlined the process of gathering the photographs for this book. Belden, a teacher at Minooka Community High School, has created two local history classes and, with those students, has published additional titles about Grundy County.

I would be remiss if I did not mention my publisher at Arcadia, Amy Perryman. She often had to talk me out of giving up along the way, when images would not work, when my scanner would not cooperate, and when I felt overwhelmed by the process. She often concluded e-mails of encouragement with the words "you got this," which was enough to get me back on track.

Lastly, I would like to thank the residents of Channahon and Minooka. In my role as a local editor of Channahon-Minooka.Patch.com, they have told me stories of the towns. For instance, I knew about the incorporation, unincorporation, and re-incorporation of the Village of Channahon long before I began this book. That story, and the one about what is now McKinley Woods once being a CCC camp, made the idea of writing this type of history appealing to me. Special thanks go to Joe Cook and Missy Schumacher, whose stories sent me in search of photographs to share.

Unless otherwise indicated, the photographs in this book were provided by the Three Rivers Public Library local history collection. In addition to the persons and institutions already mentioned, a variety of online sources were used in researching this book, including county, state, and university resources.

INTRODUCTION

Although Channahon and Minooka sit side by side, they are very different villages. What they share, though, are their foundings based on the promise of jobs. For Channahon, job creation came via the Illinois & Michigan (I&M) Canal. In Minooka, the railroads passing through the village drew the first residents. Minooka had three railroads, the Rock Island, the Interurban, and the Chicago, Ottawa & Peoria Electric Line. Minooka was the highest point on the Rock Island Line; the railroad eventually lowered the tracks through town because trains were struggling to make the incline. Today, the Rock Island tracks, which run adjacent to Main Street in Minooka, remain lower than street level. They are still used by freight trains that roll through the town. In Channahon, the I&M Canal drove people to settle the area. Strangely, the canal, or, rather, a bridge over the canal, resulted in a change to the village's legal status. After a bridge over the I&M Canal failed while a car was traversing it, the owner of the car threatened to sue the village. To avoid legal troubles, the village became unincorporated. It reverted to its prior status in 1961.

The history of the area is that of rural America. Prominent in this book are photographs of country schools. Such schools dotted the countryside and were primarily one-room schoolhouses that took in children from the surrounding farmland. In Channahon, many of the early settlers either built the I&M Canal or were employed in maintaining it. The village of Channahon also had a CCC camp in what is now McKinley Woods, more than 300 acres of land owned by the Forest Preserve of Will County. The men in that camp also worked on the I&M Canal. Minooka had its own hotel, the Minooka Hotel, which later went by the names Union Hotel and Schiek Hotel. The building survived into the 1960s.

Unlike Channahon, Minooka, with its historic downtown, looks very much as it did when it was first settled. Although restaurants have taken over what used to be bank buildings, the downtown looks very much the same. Another aspect of the town's continuity is that the grain elevator, on the south side of the street, not only still stands, it is a functioning facility.

Both towns have done a good job of preserving and/or reusing historic buildings. The building that served as the second Minooka School, a two-story brick building, is part of a larger structure that serves as the Minooka Primary Center. In Channahon, Pioneer Path School has a smaller, older building that is part of the larger structure.

Both towns also had their own Masonic lodges. The building that housed the Masonic lodge in Minooka now serves as the Minooka Branch of the Three Rivers Public Library. The building also houses the local history collection in the basement.

Before Channahon and Minooka were named and incorporated, the area featured other early settlements. Old buildings still stand in Dresden, which also has a settlers' cemetery and a mule barn. These structures are now part of Dollinger Family Farm, an attraction that is open to the public during certain times of the year. For the past couple of years, the mule barn has been part of a haunted house attraction. The Aux Sable settlement does not have any surviving buildings, but a settlers' cemetery remains. Aux Sable Cemetery, a garden cemetery, is surrounded on three sides by trees. There is only one entrance and one exit to the cemetery.

Today, Channahon and Minooka are independent villages. Channahon serves as a bedroom community for much of the population. They own houses or rent in Channahon, but they work in other communities. For these people, the hope is that Channahon will see more commercial development, especially a grocery store. While some residents of the village of Minooka work elsewhere, they are generally working closer to home than are the residents of Channahon.

One

RAILROADS

The Chicago, Rock Island & Pacific Railroad (CRI&P) eventually became the Rock Island Line. Minooka was founded as a result of the railroads, which brought settlers in the form of employees and those needed to operate the local amenities. Minooka had its own hotel to serve the visitors who came by railroad. The CRI&P depot in Minooka is shown here.

The Rock Island Line ran east and west through town. Its tracks, which had to be lowered, are used today by freight trains.

Shown here is the original Rock Island station in Minooka. The original tracks were laid in 1852. The line included two sets of eastbound tracks and two sets of westbound tracks.

These present-day photographs show the railroad tracks that run through Minooka. To this day, the tracks are lower than street level. Visible above is the building that once housed the blacksmith shop. Below is the still-operational grain elevator. The photograph was taken looking west from the parking lot that is adjacent to the tracks. On Saturdays in the summer, the lot is the site of a local farmers' market. (Both photographs by Dawn Aulet.)

Shown here is the station for the Interurban line, which was another name for the Chicago, Ottawa & Peoria Electric Line. Established in 1909, the line ran between Joliet and Depue, Illinois. On Sundays, extra cars were attached to the trains, as people came to Minooka to watch horse racing at the racetrack on the south edge of the village. The three-story building in the background is the Union or Hamilton House Hotel. The building stood at the corner of Wabena Avenue and Wapella Street from 1858 until the early 1960s.

These flyers, passed out by the Rock Island Line, offered suburban timetables as well as information regarding vacations to Colorado by train. The flyer at left states that the trains arrive and depart from LaSalle Station in Chicago. Passengers had a choice to travel by coach or Pullman car, or via an all-expense tour, which, according to the information in the image below, were escorted.

14

Two

I&M CANAL

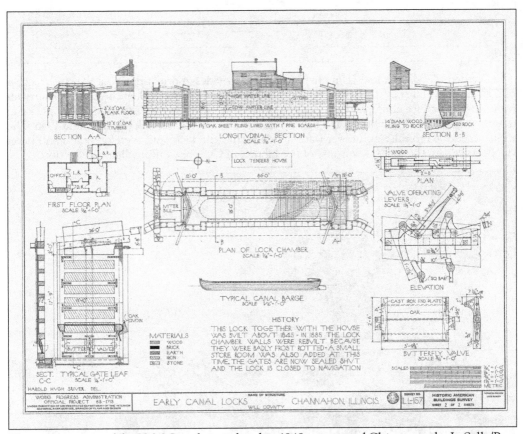

The construction of the I&M Canal, completed in 1848, connected Chicago to the LaSalle/Peru area of Illinois. The canal was 96 miles in length and ran through the village of Channahon. It is the reason that most early settlers of the village sought a home there. (Courtesy of the Library of Congress online digital collection.)

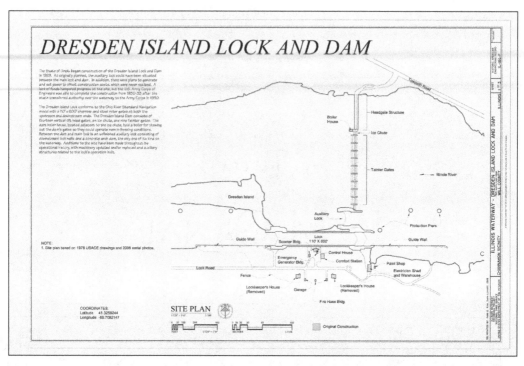

DRESDEN ISLAND LOCK AND DAM

The State of Illinois began construction of the Dresden Island Lock and Dam in 1929. As originally planned, the auxiliary lock would have been situated between the main lock and dam. In addition, there were plans to generate and sell power to offset construction costs, which were never realized. A lack of funds hampered progress at the site, but the U.S. Army Corps of Engineers was able to complete the construction from 1930-33 after the state transferred authority over the waterway to the Army Corps in 1930.

The Dresden Island Lock conforms to the Ohio River Standard Navigation model with a 110' x 600' chamber and steel miter gates at both the upstream and downstream ends. The Dresden Island Dam consists of fourteen vertical-lift head gates, an ice chute, and nine Tainter gates. The dam boiler house, located adjacent to the ice chute, held a boiler for thawing out the dam's gates so they could operate even in freezing conditions. Between the dam and main lock is an unfinished auxiliary lock consisting of downstream lock walls and a concrete arch dam, the only one of its kind on the waterway. Additions to the site have been made throughout its operational history, with machinery updated and/or replaced and auxiliary structures related to the lock's operation built.

NOTE:
1. Site plan based on 1978 USACE drawings and 2006 aerial photos.

COORDINATES:
Latitude   41.3259244
Longitude -88.7082147

SITE PLAN

The Dresden Island Lock and Dam site plan (above) provides information about the construction of the dam. The state began construction in 1929. The Dresden Island Dam consists of 14 vertical-lift head gates, an ice chute, and a boiler for thawing out the dam's gates so they could operate in freezing conditions. The photograph below shows the open locks at lock No. 6 around 1936. The locks functioned to raise and lower water levels within the lock and, therefore, raise and lower the boats within the locks. (Courtesy of the Library of Congress online digital collection.)

Shown here are locks No. 6 and No. 7 as well as the lock tender's house. This particular house no longer stands.

This photograph shows the Aux Sable Locks on the I&M Canal, off of Cemetery Road. The building visible at center is gone.

Channahon State Park is the site of two locks and a restored lock tender's house (shown here). Only three lock tenders' houses remain. One is in Channahon, another is in Lockport, and one stands at the Aux Sable access, which is between Channahon and Morris. (Courtesy of the Library of Congress online digital collection.)

This area of the I&M Canal is located in Channahon State Park. Seen here in 1936, the site looks much the same today. (Courtesy of the Library of Congress online digital collection.)

The above photograph, taken in 1936, depicts someone operating a lock on the I&M Canal. All of the canal's locks were hand-operated. The lock tenders were responsible for a variety of tasks, including operating the locks, recording water levels, and making sure that tolls were paid. The below photograph provides a close-up of the lock's mechanism. The lever system is evident. (Courtesy of the Library of Congress online digital collection.)

When the I&M Canal was designed and built, it required 15 locks to operate. This photograph, taken in May 1936, shows lock No. 6 at what is now Channahon State Park in Channahon. (Courtesy of the Library of Congress online digital collection.)

This is the south elevation and south gate of lock No. 6 on the I&M Canal in Channahon. (Courtesy of the Library of Congress online digital collection.)

Three

CHURCHES

This is the original St. Mary's Church, which was located on what is now Ridge Road in Minooka. This building lasted from 1865 until 1903, when it was struck by lightning and burned down. As the story goes, a conductor on the Elgin, Joliet & Eastern Railroad first saw the fire. He blew his whistle again and again until someone woke up. Despite a bucket brigade, the building burned to the ground.

Catholic Church, Minooka. Ill.

39312.

This c. 1909 photograph depicts St. Mary's Catholic Church in its current location on St. Mary's Street. When plans were made to rebuild the church, it was moved from what is now Ridge Road adjacent to St. Mary's Cemetery to St. Mary's Street, where it stands today. The physical move situated the church within the village of Minooka. Despite the fact that the original church burned to the ground, the pastor at the time, Father Joseph McMahon, saved the baptism and marriage records. Additionally, the original sanctuary lamp, which hangs above the altar in the current building, was saved by a parishioner. The new church was dedicated on October 4, 1904. Father McMahon served the parish until his death in 1928, at which point Father Armand Martin was appointed pastor. This photograph is the front side of a postcard dated December 15, 1914.

This is the reverse of the postcard, dated December 15, 1914, that is featured on the previous page. It is addressed to a resident of Minooka named Anna. Although it is hard to see in the image, the back of this postcard would have had a line down the center. Postcards with divided backs were produced between 1907 and 1914. This was the golden era of postcards, with consumption in the United States increasing greatly. At this time, too, the center of postcard printing shifted. Germany, formerly the center of postcard production, gave way to England and the United States. In response to the beginning of World War I, postage for a postcard was raised, from 1¢ to 2¢. When the war ended, in 1918, the cost to mail a postcard returned to 1¢.

This photograph of St. Mary's Catholic Church in Minooka was taken around 1907. The new building had been dedicated two years earlier, in 1905. After the first church had been hit by lightning, the entire village came together to help erect the new building. Parishioners at St. Mary's joined with the congregation of Minooka United Methodist Church to construct another building. This kindness was repaid about 10 years later when the Minooka United Methodist Church building was struck by a tornado in 1917. The Methodist church was completely destroyed. The congregation of St. Mary's stepped up and helped the Methodist congregation rebuild their church. The pulpit at St. Mary's was designed after the pulpit at the Methodist church. The church's current location is in a residential neighborhood a couple of blocks from a school and about two blocks from the downtown area of the village.

This postcard of St. Mary's in Minooka has a good deal of writing on it. On the right, the photographer wrote "St. Mary's Church Minooka, Ill." Photographers could write directly on the negative and often had their own numbering system. Each reproduction of the photograph thus had the same handwritten label. In this case, the reproduction was in the form of a postcard. A note written on the left by the sender reads, "Hello Girlie, does this look familiar? Now will you laugh at me when I tell you I will send you a souvenir postal of Minooka? Lola and I were in town this P.M., pretty nearly froze coming home. It will soon be time to go to skating parties." The postcard was addressed to Miss Grace M. Steele, in Joliet.

This is the first building that housed the Minooka United Methodist Church. The church was created in 1856 and met in Ferguson's store, which was located on Mondamin and Osceola Streets. It was moved to the school before the congregation erected this first building in 1866.

nooka M.E. church.
Before 1917

In 1939, the name of the church was changed, from Methodist Episcopal to Methodist. In 1968, the name was again changed, from Methodist to Minooka United Methodist Church.

This is another view of the original Minooka United Methodist Church building. The photograph was reproduced into a postcard. The copy is dated April 26 and is addressed to Mrs. Anna Ferguson in Chicago. Although there is no year on the card, it can be determined based on the design of the back that it was produced between 1907 and 1914, although the 1¢ stamp indicates it must have been produced a couple of years earlier. The text reads: "Anna, how are you when ever you want more eggs return the crate and I will send you it full The men are at work on the steele truck the fruit trees are full of blossoms hope there will be some fruit." The writing cuts off at this point, but it looks to be signed, "Mother."

The Minooka Methodist Church was destroyed by a tornado in 1917. Although it had been more than a decade since a lightning strike destroyed St. Mary's Church, the congregation that was helped by the Methodist Church assisted the Methodist congregation rebuild. Unlike St. Mary's, though, the Methodist congregation chose to rebuild the church on the same site as the original structure, on what is now Church Street in Minooka. The back of the photograph, pictured below, states, "ruins of Minooka M.E. Church 1917, after cyclone." The tornado outbreak that year killed 382 people.

ruins of Minooka
M.E. Church
1917, afte
cyclone.

M 1992-16

This is a photograph of the second Minooka United Methodist Church building, which was completed in December 1917. The building, made of brick, does not resemble the church's previous incarnation. Construction on this building began the day after the other structure was destroyed. Church members, including members of the ladies guild, joined the efforts to salvage materials to be reused. Despite the fact that the building was destroyed by tornado, the bell from the 1866 building survived. It was hung in the tower in 1917, but was removed in 1972 due to leaks in the building.

The second building of the Minooka United Methodist church is seen here before renovations in 1982. The stained-glass windows visible here were given in memory of a doctor, a blacksmith, a prominent businessman, a war hero, a minister, a little girl, a little boy, and another minister and his wife. In 1972, the church was repaired, and the bell was removed from the tower. In 1982, though, the church saw an expansion of the sanctuary. The building is still located on Church Street.

In 1982, the Minooka United Methodist Church underwent a significant renovation. The sanctuary was expanded to its present dimensions. Throughout the years, the church has seen a number of improvements and changes. In 1949, the annex was built as a school bus garage. The land, originally owned by the church, was sold to the school district and was repurchased by the church in 1968. By 1973, the site was converted into a youth room, kitchen, and dining and meeting hall. The church plans to continue to grow. In September 2001, the church purchased land in southwest Minooka bordering Ridge Road. With an additional donation, a total of 15 acres was acquired, and Minooka United Methodist Church plans to erect a new building on that land in the coming years.

The original parsonage of the Minooka United Methodist Church was built in 1868. In 1989, a new brick parsonage was built, with the members of the church completing most of the labor. The new parsonage took six months to build. The old building was sold and moved south, on the other side of the railroad on Wapella Street. It is now a private home. When the parsonage was moved, residents came out to see the proceedings. There was concern that the building, more than a century old, would not survive the move.

The original bell on the Minooka United Methodist Church survived the tornado that leveled the building in 1917. It was housed in the bell tower until 1972, when it was removed due to leaks. The bell was stored on the Holt farm until July 4, 1976, when it was placed in its current location, the west side of the church building. (Photograph by Dawn Aulet.)

The original St. Mary's Cemetery is along what is now Ridge Road in Minooka. The cemetery remains much as it has throughout its history, but retail and industry have built up around it. From inside the cemetery, visible to the south is the McDonalds sign, built to be seen from nearby Interstate 80. The scene provides an interesting contrast between history and progress. (Photographs by Dawn Aulet.)

St. Mary's Church in Minooka has been in its current location, on St. Mary's Street, since 1904. The year before, the original church, which was located on what is now Ridge Road in Minooka, was destroyed by fire resulting from a lightning strike. The sanctuary lamp and baptism and marriage records were rescued from the blaze. In 1990, the church caught fire a second time. And, for a second time, the sanctuary lamp was rescued. (Photographs by Dawn Aulet.)

The Minooka United Methodist Church, seen here as it appears today, is located across the street from the Minooka Primary Center, which is also a historical building. The church, which has seen its share of expansions over the years, offers a food pantry for local residents and serves as one of the village warming shelters in winter months. (Photograph by Dawn Aulet.)

Four

SCHOOLS

The original Minooka School was located on Massasoit and Church Streets. It was taken down in 1924, when Minooka erected a larger building. The second building, a brick two-story structure facing Massasoit Street, can still be seen as the central part of the building that now serves as the Minooka Primary Center. As was the style in those days, the photographer wrote a sequential number (11209) on the negative, seen on this postcard.

Post Card

Dear Agatha – This is where I received my edu. Have not been so I could write a letter. Hope you are enjoying your vacation to the limit. Your letter was very interesting and was certainly glad to receive it. Have been here since Tues. eve. Mary.

Miss Agatha Schneider

Nadams Grove,

Illinois

This is the back of the postcard of the original Minooka School seen on the previous page. The postcard is addressed to a woman named Agatha and says, "Dear Agatha, this is where I received my edu. Have not been so I could write a letter. Hope you are enjoying your education to the limit. Your letter was very interesting and was certainly glad to receive it. Have been here since Tues. evening." The card is signed "Mary."

This is the original schoolhouse in Channahon. The building occupied the present location of Pioneer Path School. The two-story building, on Route 6 and Tryon Street, was erected in 1869 for $18,000. It accommodated students from elementary grades to the second year of high school. It burned down in the 1920s.

The above photograph shows the Minooka School around 1924. In the left background can be seen the building that now serves as the Minooka Primary Center. In the photograph at left, people walk on a sidewalk in front of the Minooka School. The original Minooka School was razed in 1924. The two-story brick structure at the center of the current building was the replacement for the original school.

The building in both these images now serves as the Minooka Primary Center. The center of the building is the second Minooka School, the two-story brick structure. The school district uses the facility for early childhood and kindergarten instruction. When it was originally built, it was the only school in the village and housed all grades.

This photograph shows the rear of the Minooka Primary Center. The building is across the street from the Minooka United Methodist Church. It currently houses the Minooka Primary Center as well as the superintendent's office.

This was the second building to house Walley School. The original building was erected in the 1800s, but fell into disrepair and fell apart later in the 1800s. The second building still stands and is a private residence today.

A student holds the American flag outside Walley School. This is the second Walley School, built after the first one fell down. A family settled the area where Walley School stood, along Frontage Road. At that time, many small country schools dotted the landscape. This was one of those schools.

A student and what seems to be an instructor pose in front of Walley School. The building still stands, and is now a private residence, located on Frontage Road adjacent to Interstate 80. It is still recognizable because of its diamond-shaped windows.

In these photographs, students and teachers pose outside of Walley School. The tradition at the time was to bring the classes outside once a year to take a group photograph. Pictured above in no particular order are Virginia Hetall, Tommy Marau, Wesley Roswold, Vance Vaksdall, Dennis Gjerde, Paul Roswold, Thomas Hextall, Janet Dewey, Joyce Hextall, Nancy Hextall and Miss Tess McFernan. Both photographs are dated 1947 and signed "Mary Talbot" in the bottom right corner.

Students in these photographs are standing outside Dresden School. The building, on Route 6 and McLinden Road, was torn down in the 1960s when Route 6 was widened.

Students pose outside of Aux Sable School. The school was part of the Aux Sable settlement, which was situated along the Aux Sable aqueduct off Cemetery and Tabler Roads. It is now an unincorporated area. The reverse of this photograph, dated 1935, states the school was along Cemetery Road.

The children shown here are Aux Sable School students. The reverse of the photograph lists the names Joe Rene Ehrman, S. Kinsella, Berneice Rose, Faye Bell, Freddy Swiggett, Marie Kinkin, Ruth Boardman, and Turner Hansen.

Among the students shown here are Jo Rene Ehrmann, S. Kinsella, R. Boardman, F. Bell, E. Blankenship, M. Kinkin, and B. Friddle. The photograph is dated 1950.

Students of the Aux Sable School pose for the camera. The back of this photograph lists the boys' names, in no particular order, as Raymond Boardman, Turner Hansen, Donnie Memper, and Freddy Swiggert. The photograph is dated 1950.

The reverse side of this photograph lists the following students: M. Kinkin, E. Blankenship, B. Friddle, B. Boardman, B. Rose, F. Bell, J. Ehrman, and ? Blankenship.

This photograph of students at Aux Sable School shows what looks to be a class play. The signs at the back of the stage read "Now is the time to be careful," and "Be wise and always put safety first." A child dressed as a police officer holds a stop sign in front of a child sitting in a car. The date handwritten on the bottom of the photograph is cut off, but appears to be 1931.

Brown School students pose in front of the building in December 1934 (above) and 1935 (below). Brown School, a country school, was located on Minooka and Brown Roads. It is believed that the building was erected around 1837. It has since been torn down.

These photographs of students at Brown School are dated April 1935. The school stood at Minooka and Brown Roads. Brown School may have been the first to be built in the area.

Minooka School stood where the Minooka Primary Center is today. The original building was replaced in 1924. Part of it was moved and became a house, which has since been torn down. The sign in this photograph identifies the students as members of Room 2, posing in 1906.

In keeping with the era's tradition, the entire school has gathered outside. Schools would often have one photograph taken per year. This looks to be the entire population of Minooka School.

In this 1912 photograph, students of Minooka School pose for a class portrait.

Minooka School students pose on the steps in this undated photograph.

By the time this photograph was taken in 1936, the original Minooka School had been replaced by the building that is now part of the Minooka Primary Center. The second building was a brick two-story structure. All grades attended this school, which, like most schools of the era, extended only to the sophomore year of high school.

This barn served as the gym for Minooka School students. It stood on the corner of Massasoit and Mondamin Streets. Many students complained about how cold and drafty the barn was. It was torn down prior to the school's expansion, which included a gymnasium, in the 1950s.

Sixth-grade students at Pioneer Path School in Channahon pose for a photograph in 1973. Shown are, from left to right, (first row) Donna Lawrence, Bob Loskill, Linda Morris, Diane Haga, Ginselle LaRose, and Stephanie Jensen; (second row), Brenda Spier, Anita Roller, Steve Gallion, Scott Hammitt, Marilyn Mecha, Carrie Sak, and Mr. Mahoney; (third row), Kay Monk, Rhonda Lehman, John Zelko, George McCoy, Mark Turner, Herby Fishburn, Pam Borella, and Mark McCraken; (fourth row), Bruce McMillin, Lori Lawson, Roseanne McClintock, Sherrie Anderson, Carrie Anderson, Kristie Towles, Beth Ann Hawkins, and Gordon Baker.

This building, at the site of the original Minooka School, has seen a number of additions and renovations over the years. It is seen here in the evening with the front lights on. When it became the Minooka Primary Center in 2011, many renovations were undertaken. Prior to its current use, it was the Minooka Intermediate School, and before that, Minooka Junior High. (Photograph by Dawn Aulet.)

The 1955 graduation at Channahon School is seen here. The original Channahon School is part of the building at what is now Pioneer Path School, on Route 6 and Tryon Street.

Five

MINOOKA

Shown here is the home owned by Leander and Dolly Smith. The house was on St. Mary's Street and Wabena Avenue. Dolly Smith is credited with providing the village of Minooka with its name, as well as the names of all the streets in town. Smith spoke Potawatamie, although it is not known if she had any ties with the tribe. The back of the photograph reads: "Mr. Dan Halls home, Minooka, Ill. Brick house there now owned by J.W. Crook, 1928." Another note on the photograph reads, "this house was torn down and a brick home built."

This is the original Masonic hall, which stood on St. Mary's Street and Wabena Avenue. The building was partially destroyed by a tornado shortly after it was erected in 1924. Prior to its construction, a one-story structure on the same site served as the Masonic lodge.

This building serves the community as the Three Rivers Public Library, Minooka Branch. The building was renovated in 1992. (Photograph by Dawn Aulet)

MORRIS, ILL.

This toboggan slide stood in Minooka at the corner of Church and Osceola Streets. A.K. Knapp, who had no children of his own, installed the slide every year for the children of the village to enjoy. The slide began to deteriorate, however, and after Knapp passed away in 1904, it was not replaced.

Shown here is the building that was the blacksmith shop. It still stands at the corner of Wapella Street and Wabena Avenue. The shop was founded by S.A. Ferguson in 1880. Along with providing blacksmith services, Ferguson built wagons and carriages and completed general repairs.

The building that was once Ferguson's blacksmith shop still stands at the corner of Wapella Street and Wabena Avenue. There is a beam across the front window and door that reads "Ferguson Blacksmith."

The above photograph shows the line to the grain elevator in Minooka. The elevator, which still stands and continues to operate, is one of the landmarks of the village. The postcard (below) is addressed to a Miss Emma Ferguson in Iowa.

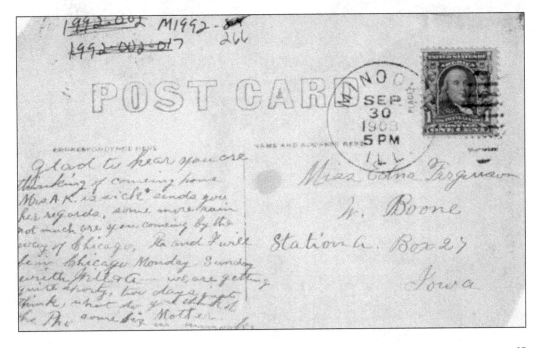

This building in downtown Minooka has seen a number of incarnations, including a bank (above), the village post office, and numerous restaurants (below). It currently houses a seafood restaurant that serves Illinois wines.

Looking E. on Main St., Minooka, Ill.   39307.

The prominent building in this street scene is a mercantile store. The photograph is looking east on Main Street. The back of the photograph reads, "Mondamin east from Massasoit." Visible at center is the original Minooka water tower, which is no longer standing.

STATEMENT

The Farmers' First National Bank of Minooka

At the Close of Business August 31, 1918, Condensed From

Report to Comptroller of Currency

RESOURCES		LIABILITIES	
Loans and discounts	$179,517.78	Capital stock	$ 25,000.00
Overdrafts	364.19		
United States Bonds	45,000.00	Surplus and Profits	21,686.58
Other bonds and securities	14,605.57		
Stock in Federal Reserve Bank	1,450.00	Circulation	25,000.00
Banking house and fixtures	8,000.00		
Redemption	1,250.00	Miscellaneous items	1,522.00
CASH AND DUE FROM BANKS	39,992.54	DEPOSITS	216,971.50
	$290,180.08		$290,180.08

This is a receipt from the Farmers First National Bank of Minooka. The bank had numerous locations in town, including the building in downtown Minooka with the rounded window seen on the opposite page.

The Electric Theater in Minooka was on Mondamin Street. Little is known of its history.

In this undated photograph, people stand on the porch of the Union Hotel. It was also known as the Hamilton House Hotel and the Shiek Hotel.

The Hamilton House Hotel, which later was called the Minooka Union Hotel and then the Shiek Hotel, was constructed in 1858. The hotel, designed by C.V. Hamilton, was located near the train depot on the southeast corner of Wapella Street and Wabena Avenue. The three-story structure stood until the early 1960s and included approximately 20 rooms. The third floor of the hotel housed a large dance room where the first Minooka High School basketball game was played.

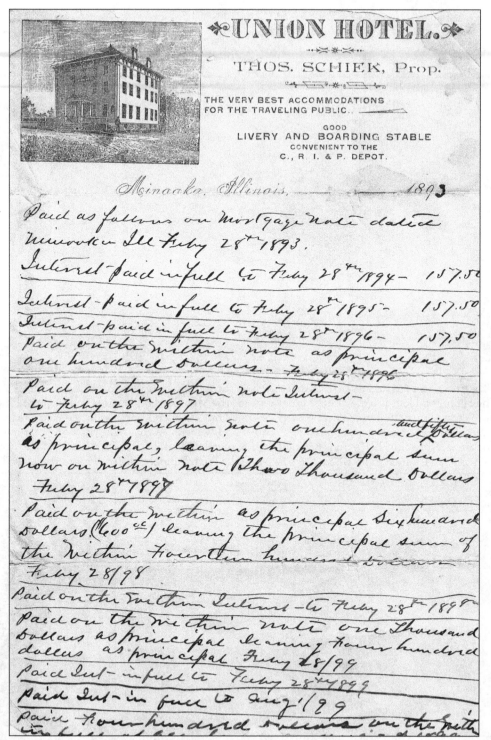

✲UNION HOTEL.✲

THOS. SCHIEK, Prop.

THE VERY BEST ACCOMMODATIONS
FOR THE TRAVELING PUBLIC.

GOOD
LIVERY AND BOARDING STABLE
CONVENIENT TO THE
C., R. I. & P. DEPOT.

Minooka, Illinois, _____ 189 3

Paid as follows on mortgage note dated
Minooka Ill Feby 28th 1893.

Interest paid in full to Feby 28th 1894 – 157.50

Interest paid in full to Feby 28th 1895 – 157.50

Interest paid in full to Feby 28th 1896 – 157.50
Paid on the within note as principal
one hundred Dollars – Feby 28 1896

Paid on the within note Interest –
to Feby 28th 1897

Paid on the within note one hundred and fifty Dollars
as principal, leaving the principal sum
now on within note Three Thousand Dollars
Feby 28th 1897

Paid on the within as principal Six hundred
Dollars ($600.00) leaving the principal sum of
the within Fourteen hundred dollars
Feby 28/98

Paid on the within Interest to Feby 28th 1898
Paid on the within note one Thousand
Dollars as principal leaving Four hundred
dollars as principal Feby 28/99
Paid Int in full to Feby 28th 1899

Paid Int in full to Aug 1/99
Paid Four hundred dollars on the within

This is a sheet of stationery from the Union Hotel. The letterhead, printed at the top, reads "Union Hotel, Thos. Shiek, Prop. The very best accommodations for the traveling public. Good livery and boarding stable convenient to the C.R.I.&P. depot."

70

The original water tower in the village of Minooka was built in 1906. It was taken down in 2007, having fallen into disuse for some time. The tower, made out of redwood, was replaced with a metal tower in the same location.

Shown here is the second incarnation of the Minooka water tower. It was brought to Minooka from the Pullman neighborhood in Chicago, which shares a railroad history with the village of Minooka. The neighborhood was built in the 1880s by George Pullman for his Pullman Palace Car Company. In 1897, the town, which was owned by the Pullman Company, was ordered to be sold and was eventually annexed into the city of Chicago. This water tower was taken down within the last five years.

71

These photographs show Main Street in Minooka. In the below photograph, looking west, window signs can be easily read, including Frank Wilson's Meat Market and Ward's Bakery.

These photographs of Mondamin Street looking west from Wapella provide more distant views of the downtown area. Minooka's downtown area includes a historic grain elevator, which functions and sells grain to this day and supports small businesses, from a T-shirt shop to restaurants.

This photograph looking north on Massasoit Street was taken between 1907 and 1910.

Beehives used to dot the fields at the honey farm on Route 6. It is now an industrial area filled with factories.

This is a photograph of the foundry in Minooka. The building on Mondamin Street burned down a few years ago. When in operation, the business did metalwork and repaired farm equipment.

This is the A.K. Knapp House. Knapp owned Minooka Grain and Lumber and was a charter member of the Farmers First National Bank. The home is currently located on Osceola and St. Mary's Streets. The home was built in 1870 and features about 4,000 square feet of living space.

Six

CHANNAHON

Shown here is Channahon's Masonic hall. Lodge No. 262 was chartered in Channahon in 1857 and included about 50 members.

Shown here is a river scene in the village of Channahon. The Des Plaines River, and especially the I&M Canal, were the major factors in the establishment of Channahon.

The bridge shown in the postcard above was in Channahon. The reverse of the postcard, seen below, was signed by R. Johnson.

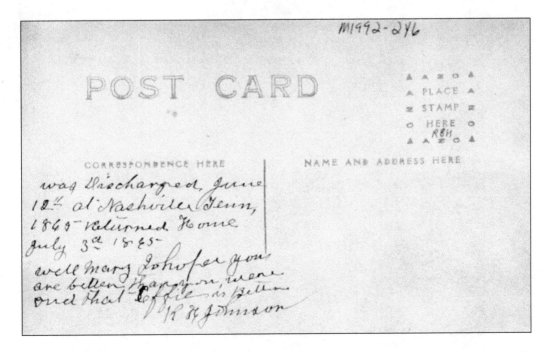

The bridges in the village of Channahon hold rich histories. The bridge above looks structurally sound as a buggy makes its way across. But it was the collapse of a bridge (below) while a car was on it that ended the original incorporation of Channahon. The owner of the car threatened to sue the village over the faulty bridge. In order to avoid being sued and losing significant funds, the village chose unincorporation. It was re-incorporated in 1962.

Channanhon State Park, shown here in winter, houses lock No. 6 of the I&M Canal. It is now owned by the state of Illinois. In a previous effort to save the park, the village owned it for a short time.

This bridge is located at lock No. 7 of the I&M Canal. There are three locks along the canal within the village limits of Chananhon.

Du Page River Dam, Channahon State Park, Channahon, Illinois

The DuPage River Dam at Channahon State Park (above) formerly offered residents a place to swim. Now, fishermen wade into the waters, but swimming is not allowed. The field in the photograph below is located at Channahon State Park.

The boys in this photograph are sitting on a bar of a lock at Channahon State Park. The park continues to be a destination for families. Hiking and biking paths connect trails through multiple counties. The park also offers camping. Channahon means "the meeting of the waters." In this case, the DuPage, Des Plaines, and Kankakee Rivers, all of which meet within village limits. The area became a state park in 1932.

The area now known as McKinley Woods, a 525-acre property maintained by the Forest Preserve of Will County, was once home to a Civilian Conservation Corps camp. Camp Brandon housed men who worked on the I&M Canal. The Forest Preserve of Will County gradually acquired the property between 1931 and 2004. Today, the land is adjacent to a number of housing developments and is used recreationally by residents and visitors alike. (Above, courtesy of Three Rivers Public Library local history collection; below, photograph by Dawn Aulet.)

The above photograph shows the Knowlton Home in Channahon. The reverse of the photograph (pictured at right) reads "Taken by Jay Jenks, 1912. Our house in Channahon where I was born."

William and Ada Knowlton were photographed in 1913 along the DuPage River south of Channahon.

Construction on the Manor Motel began in 1946, and it opened in 1954. It was an original stop along Route 66. The motel still stands, as does the building across the street that served as a supper club of sorts. The motel even offered swimming lessons for community members. (Above, courtesy of Three Rivers Public Library local history collection; below, photograph by Dawn Aulet.)

Two men stand next to a vehicle belonging to the Emiley Cabinet Shop. Little is known of the shop, which was based in Channahon.

Seven

PEOPLE

The people in this 1938 photograph are posing outside of the Gleaners Hall. The building stood on Sandwich Road near Cemetery Road in Aux Sable Township. Gleaners Hall was gone by the 1960s. It is not known what caused its demise.

The above photograph shows what looks to be a wedding. It was held at the Masonic hall in Channahon. The back of the photograph (below) lists seven names, but they are not legible. The photograph was taken by C.V. Hultberg, 422 South Fourth Street in Aurora, on November 20, 1950.

Eastern Star

334-1
C.V. HULTBERG
422 S. FOURTH
AURORA, ILL. PHONE 2-4555
NOV 20 1950

Harvey Vaksdal - Preacher
Fannie Matteson
Stacy Matteson
Roy Hare
Virginia Vaksdal
Ella Hare
Mildred Coody

The above photograph was taken during the wedding depicted on the opposite page at the Masonic lodge. A Masonic symbol is visible in the background. The reverse of the photograph lists seven names, but the ink has been damaged over the years, rendering the names difficult to read.

Ella McKanna

Dorothy Johnke

Edna Bell

Virginia Vaksdal

Jock McKanna

Irey Holt

Vera Lewis

Luanna Seitsinger

Flo Davis

Marge Heap

Harvey Vaksdal

Betti Patten

3rd row

Roy Hare

Ethel Tabler

Mildred Cosby

Virginia Steiger

Lottie Smith

Helen Blair

Nadine Insler

Anna Grunback

Back row

This photograph and the ones on the following pages are of a picnic for the Brown School, one of many country schools that dotted the countryside. Eventually, those schools either closed or consolidated into a single district that served a larger area.

The above photograph was taken in 1937 at the Brown School picnic. The school was located in a pasture on Brown Road south of Minooka Road. The school was built about a year before the photograph below was taken.

Shown here are attendees at the Brown School picnic. Schools in these days would gather once a year for a picnic that included students' whole families. As seen on the following pages, a number of country schools had these kinds of picnics.

In this photograph, students pose at the Broadway School picnic. The Broadway School was one of the many country schools located throughout the region. Eventually, the original country schools either closed or were consolidated into larger districts.

Minooka High School basketball team members pose in this undated photograph. Today, the Minooka Community High School consists of two campuses, one in Minooka (Central Campus) and one in Channahon (South Campus). Freshmen and sophomores attend South Campus, and juniors and seniors attend Central Campus.

Shown above is a 1912 Minooka baseball team. The team members' names, listed on the back of the photograph (below), are Arthur Dirst, Leo Kaffer, Fletcher Dirst, Chas. Campbell, Larry Turner, Albert Sezgel, Earl Kaffer, John Talbot, William Talbot, Harry White, and Wendel Horper.

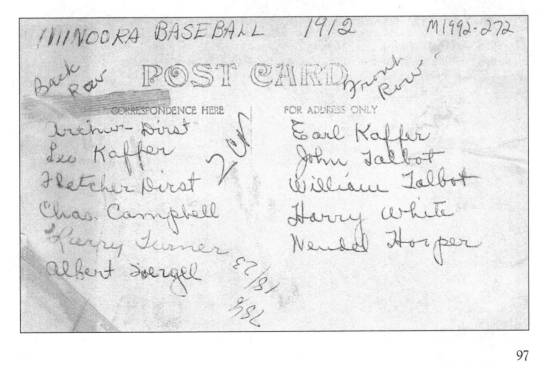

1963

Tom Harrington (2b) .263
Chuck Ryan (P) .303
Alan Borick (Lf) .2__
Dave Brown (Rf) .361
Wayne Greenbeck (Ss) ____
Don Davidson (P) .317
Larry Korek (C) .205
Don Williamson (Cf) .351
Dave Seeders (3b) .331
Tom Williamson (1b) .235

The 1963 lineup of the Minooka baseball team poses in this photograph. The team appears to be made up of adult men in the community, rather than school-age players. There were a number of these kinds of teams in the 1960s in the area. They would form a league and play each other.

Eight

POSTCARDS AND PARTIES

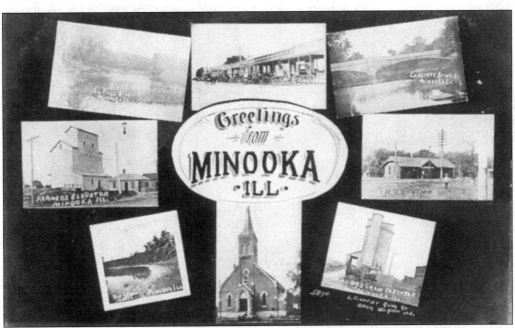

This postcard depicts a number of historical attractions to be found in Minooka. The postcard, dated 1910, was sent to Mrs. John Buckley, who lived in Minooka. The text on the back of states "To wish you, a Happy New Year." It is signed "Your friend Edna M. Bedford."

This postcard shows what looks to be a country road in Minooka. Across the bottom are the words, "Greetings from Minooka, Ill."

The front of this postcard reads, "There's something to stave off the blues in Minooka. What's your color?" The card is addressed to Marion Lunney in Seneca, Illinois. The text reads in part, "Hello Lunney, How is everything down home?" It seems to be signed "F.Y." It is dated August 4, 1914, and was sent from Minooka. The year 1914 saw the golden age of postcards move into a much more trying time for the paper form of communication. By that year, many publishers had switched from a split-back postcard to a white border postcard, a format that lasted until about 1930.

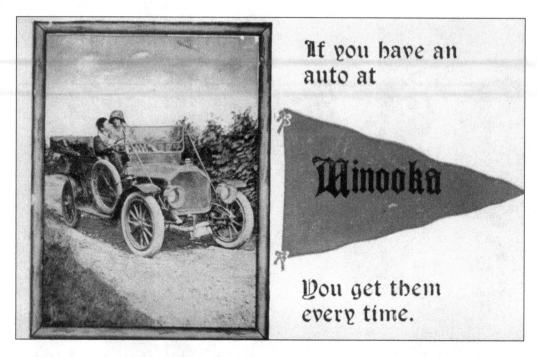

The format of this postcard resembles the one on the previous page to a great extent. The text reads, "If you have an auto at Minooka, You get them every time." The reverse of the postcard is addressed to Mrs. John Buckley, of Morris, Illinois. The message reads, "Dear Friend, was sorry to learn of your recent trouble but sincerely hope to see you walking our streets again." The last name of the sender is difficult to make out. It may be Wicly or Evich. The postcard is addressed care of a hospital.

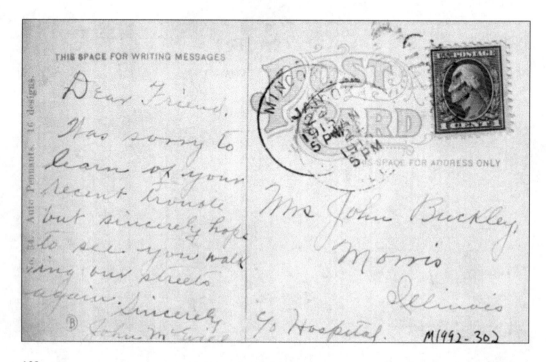

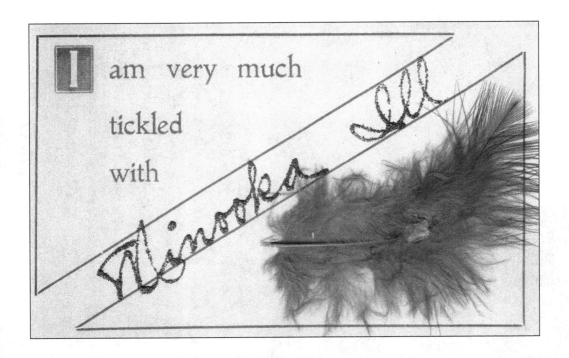

The front of this postcard, which reads, "I am very much tickled with Minooka, Ill.," had a real feather attached to it. The name of the intended recipient appears to be "Mr. Clarence Crossen." The card does not seem to have a postmark, so perhaps it was not sent. The handwritten message reads, "Wait until you come down and you will be too." It is signed "Grace."

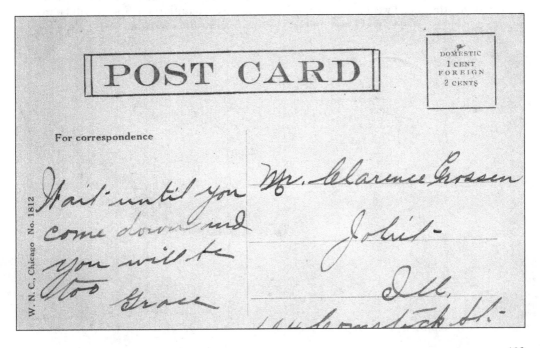

This postcard features a photograph of the Aux Sable Creek. The message, which looks to be on the front of the postcard, reads "Dec. 10 All ok. At West View and the Maples got mayo postal yesterday. Glad to hear of the safe arrival at OakRoss, warmer this morning guess the cold wave is over for the time hope we don't have another for at least a month then. Spring will be in sight to give us courage. Have a good visit and don't worry everything is alright."

Wishing Ye Good Luck
from
Minooka, Illinois

This postcard reads, "Wishing ye good luck from Minooka, Illinois." Captions in the top left identify the photographs as follows: Main Street, Corner of Massasoit and Main Street, DuPage River, and Aux Sable Creek. The postcard is stamped August 5, 1912, and is addressed to Harry A. Thayer, of El Reno, Oklahoma. The message reads "Dear Harry, Suppose we will get a letter from you this a.m. How are you making it by this time. Everyone all ok here. Nice and cool, more like Sept. than Aug. Warren Dean died last night and Ed Oakes brother was killed on the interurban." It looks to be signed, "Love Alma."

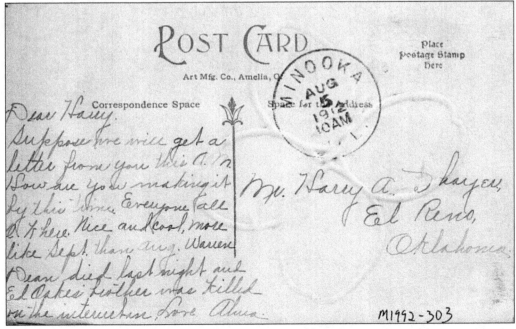

M1992-303

Greetings from MINOOKA, Ill.

The front of this postcard reads, "Greetings from Minooka, Ill." The card, sent on August 20, 1923, is addressed to Harry I. Thayer of 1619 Thirty-Third Street in Rock Island, Illinois. The message reads, "Dear Harry Boy: Many, many happy returns. Grandpa is so busy in the shop so Aunt Ollie will send a card for me."

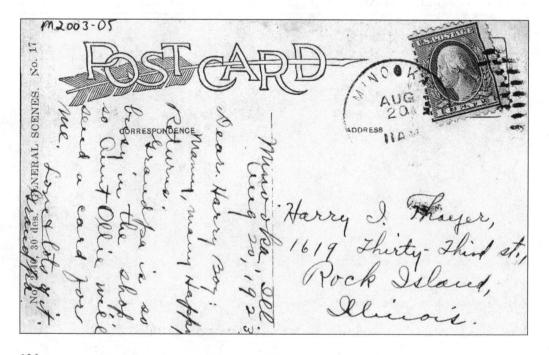

This postcard, dated December 25, 1900, features a photograph of the Minooka School. The postcard reads, "A Merry Christmas and a Happy New Year." The name on the bottom of the card looks to be Walter Goldaberry.

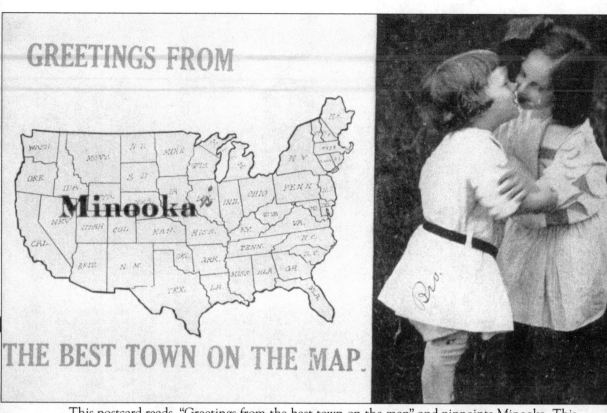

This postcard reads, "Greetings from the best town on the map" and pinpoints Minooka. This is what is known as a map postcard, which had a great following. There are groups dedicated to map postcards. Members buy, sell, trade, and discuss the cards.

A Special Day is
    set apart
To speak the love
    within the heart,
And to all Mothers
    tribute pay.
Come meet with us
on Mother's Day.
Time   May 11,- 11: A.M.
Place   Plattville Methodist
             Church

793 MADE IN U.S.A.

Mrs. William Thornton

Minooka, Illinois

%D.J. Grindle

This postcard was mailed in 1941 to a resident of Minooka, Mrs. William Thornton. The pre-printed text reads, "A special day is set apart / To speak the love within the heart, / And to all Mothers tribute pay. / Come meet with us on Mother's Day." The Mother's Day event is scheduled for 11:00 a.m. on May 11 at the Plattville Methodist Church.

Fire dances were a tradition in the village of Minooka. This is an invitation to the 10th annual fire dance. The reverse of the invitation reads "Yourself and ladies are respectfully invited to be present at the Tenth Annual Fire Dance, to be held at Central Hall, Minooka, Friday Evening, February 5th, 1897." It goes on to mention that DeLucca's Full Orchestra will perform. Tickets were $1.50, which included supper, to be furnished by Mrs. W.H. Bell. In smaller type near the bottom is the advisory that the invitation needs to be presented at the door. The following names are listed as serving on committees: J.S. Watson, C. Foster, M. Kaffer, G.T. Smith, Alex Bell, M.L. Kaffer, Frank Clark, N.J. Comerford, F. Snure, J.J. Shepley, J. Vance, C.A. Sperry, G. Colleps, H.P. Brannick, Fred Weese, Bert Ward, and C.E. Davis.

COMMITTEES:
∾⊙∾

ARRANGEMENTS:

J. S. Watson,   C. Foster,   M. Kaffer,

G. T. Smith,   Alex Bell.

INVITATION:

M. L. Kaffer,   Frank Clark,

N. J. Comerford,   F. Snure,

RECEPTION:

J. J. Shepley,   J. Vance,

C. A. Sperry,   G. Colleps.

FLOOR:

H. P. Brannick,   Fred Weese,

Bert Ward,   C. E. Davis.

Yourself and ladies are respectfully invited to

be present at the

Tenth Annual Fire Dance,

to be held at

Central Hall, Minooka,

Friday Evening, February 5th, 1897.

ooooo

DeLucca's Full Orchestra.

ooooo

Tickets, including supper, $1.50.

Supper furnished by Mrs. W. H. Bell.

Present this invitation at the door.

The 11th Annual Fire Dance was held at Schiek's Hall, which was located within the Union Hotel. The hotel was known by a number of different names over the years, including the Schiek Hotel and the Minooka Hotel. It was located on the southwest corner of Wapella Street and Wabena Avenue. The price for the dance was $1, which was 50¢ less than the price for the previous year's event. The invitation states that Leone's Full Orchestra will play. The following names are listed under committees: J.S. Watson, C. Foster, M. Kaffer, G.T. Smith, C.A. Sperry, M.L. Kaffer, Frank Clark, N.J. Comerford, J.J. Shepley, G. Colleps, H.P. Brannick, Fred Weese, C.E. Davis. E. McEvilley, J. Drumgoole, C.H. White, R.E Brady, C.A. Trowbridge, and F. Weese.

COMMITTEES:

✱ ✱

ARRANGEMENTS:

J. S. Watson,   C. Foster,   M. Kaffer,
          G. T. Smith,   C. A. Sperry.

INVITATION:

M. L. Kaffer,   Frank Clark,
          N. J. Comerford,   B. Ward.

RECEPTION:

J. J. Shepley,   W. Henry,
          C. E. Davis,   G. Colleps.

FLOOR:

H. P. Brannick,   Fred Weese,
          E. McEvilly,   J Drumgoole.

SUPPER:

C. H. White,   F. Weese,
          R. E. Brady.   C. A. Trowbridge.

Yourself and Ladies are respectfully invited to be present at the

Eleventh Annual Fire Dance

at Schiek's Hall, Minooka, Ill.,

Wednesday Evening February 2, '98.

✱ ✱ ✱ ✱

Music by Leone's Full Orchestra.

✱ ✱ ✱ ✱

Dance Tickets, $1.00.

✱ ✱ ✱ ✱

PRESENT THIS INVITATION AT THE DOOR.

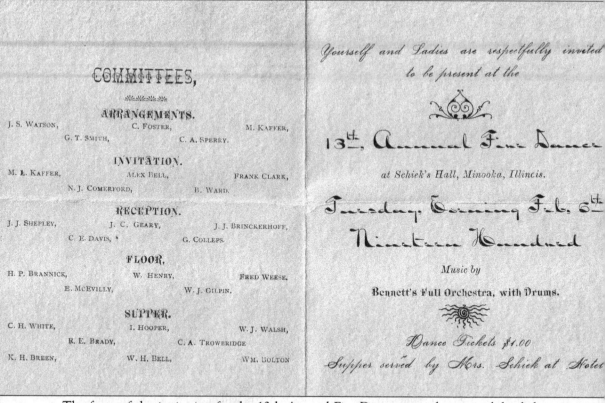

COMMITTEES,

ARRANGEMENTS.

| J. S. Watson, | C. Foster, | M. Kaffer, |
| G. T. Smith, | | C. A. Sperry. |

INVITATION.

| M. L. Kaffer, | Alex Bell, | Frank Clark, |
| N. J. Comerford, | | B. Ward. |

RECEPTION.

| J. J. Shepley, | J. C. Geary, | J. J. Brinckerhoff, |
| C. E. Davis, | | G. Colleps. |

FLOOR.

| H. P. Brannick, | W. Henry, | Fred Weese. |
| E. McEvilly, | | W. J. Gilpin. |

SUPPER.

C. H. White,	I. Hooper,	W. J. Walsh,
R. E. Brady,		C. A. Trowbridge
K. H. Breen,	W. H. Bell,	Wm. Bolton

Yourself and Ladies are respectfully invited to be present at the

13th Annual Fire Dance

at Schiek's Hall, Minooka, Illinois.

Tuesday Evening Feb. 6th Nineteen Hundred

Music by

Bennett's Full Orchestra, with Drums.

Dance Tickets $1.00

Supper served by Mrs. Schiek at Hotel

The front of the invitation for the 13th Annual Fire Dance is much more subdued than in previous years. Bennett's Full Orchestra, with drums, was to perform. The dance tickets were $1 and included dinner.

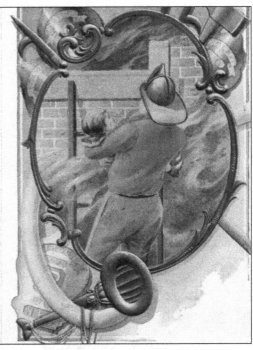

COMMITTEES

ARRANGEMENTS
J. S. Watson, C. Foster, M. Kaffer
G. T. Smith, J. J. Vana,

INVITATION
M. L. Kaffer, Alex Bell, Frank Clark,
N. J. Comerford, B. Ward,

RECEPTION
M. J. Whalen, J. C. Geary, J. J. Brinckerhoff,
C. E. Davis, G. Colleps.

FLOOR
H. P. Brannick, C. B. Chase, Fred Weese,
E. McEvilly, J J. Shepley.

SUPPER
C. H. White, I. Hooper, Jno. Wilson,
C. A. Trowbridge, D. H. Andrews.

305

For the 15th Annual Fire Dance, the invitation reverted to a much more elaborate front. The text on the invitation reads "Yourself and ladies are respectfully invited to be present at the Fifteenth Annual Fire Dance at Union Hall, Minooka, Ill. Wednesday Evening, Feb. 5th, Nineteen hundred and two. Music by Bennett's Orchestra. Dance tickets $1.00. Supper served by Mrs. Tinder."

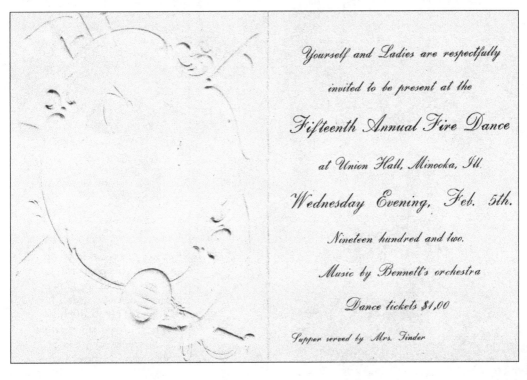

Yourself and Ladies are respectfully

invited to be present at the

Fifteenth Annual Fire Dance

at Union Hall, Minooka, Ill.

Wednesday Evening, Feb. 5th.

Nineteen hundred and two.

Music by Bennett's orchestra

Dance tickets $1.00

Supper served by Mrs. Tinder

"I Wear DOWNS' Self-Adjusting CORSETS."

A woman is depicted on the front of this postcard, an advertisement for Downs' self-adjusting corsets. The reverse of the postcard indicates that the product is for sale by Dahlem & Shepley in Minooka.

The back of the postcard shown on the previous page states, "Something New. Downs' Self Adjusting Corsets." The advertisement promises that the corset will fit any form perfectly and will not break down over the hips. It also claims that the garment is recommended by leading physicians.

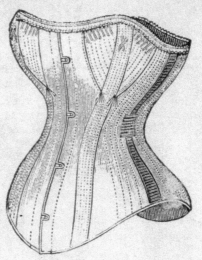

SOMETHING NEW
DOWNS'
Self Adjusting Corsets,

Constructed on Scientific and Sanitary Principles. Combining Beauty of form, COMFORT, HEALTH and DURABILITY. Made with or without Shoulder Straps and Skirt Supporting attachment.

Will fit any form perfectly and will not break down over the hips. Highly recommended by leading Physicians.

FOR SALE BY

DAHLEM & SHEPLEY,

MINOOKA, ILL.

This is another postcard advertisement for Downs' self-adjusting corsets. Again, the items are being sold by Minooka business Dahlem & Shepley.

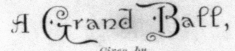

RANEE LLERO ORCHESTRA

Thanksgiving Eve. Dance

WEDNESDAY NOV. 22, 1939

MINOOKA MASONIC TEMPLE

ADM. 50c Per COUPLE   **9:00 P. M.**

The 1939 Thanksgiving Eve Dance was held at the Minooka Masonic Temple. The event cost 50¢ per couple. The Masonic lodge was located where the Three Rivers Public Library, Minooka Branch, now stands. The temple was partially destroyed by a tornado shortly after being built in 1924. Prior to the temple, a one-story building occupied the site. Pictured below is an invitation to the Grand Ball, which took place December 31, 1894. This event was also at the Minooka Masonic lodge, but was $1.50 per couple.

Yourself and Ladies are Cordially Invited to attend

A Grand Ball,

Given by

Minnehaha Chapter, No. 273, O. E. S.

Monday Evening, December 31, 1894,

at Masonic Hall, Minooka, Ill.

Grand March at 8:30.   —————   Refreshments, 11 to 12.

MUSIC BY CHAS. DORRE'S ORCHESTRA.

COMMITTEES.

ARRANGEMENT.—Mrs. A. Bell,   Mrs. C. W. Barker,   Mrs. W. H. Bell,
J. Vance.   A. Bell.

INVITATION.—Mrs. A. K. Knapp,   Mrs. H. T. Truby,   Miss Lizzie Bedford,
A. Bell,   A. E. Brown,   Miss Emma Bell.

RECEPTION.—Mrs. A. Davis,   Mrs. O. E. Searles,   Miss Ida Bedford,
J. S. Watson,   A. K. Knapp,   Miss Martha Buckley.

FLOOR.—F. J. Bedford,   C. W. Barker,   O. E. Searles,   C. E. Davis.

TICKETS, $1.50 PER COUPLE.   PRESENT THIS AT THE DOOR.

"LET ME BE YOUR RAIN-BEAU"

Wednesday Eve., June 7, 1922

AT THE

BIG DANCE

GIVEN BY THE

H AND L BOYS

CHANNAHON PAVILLION

MUSIC BY

SWEET'S 5 PIECE ORCHESTRA

Gents 75c   Ladies 35c   21   A BIG TIME FOR ALL

The village of Channahon hosted its share of parties, too. This invitation is for a big dance that took place on June 7, 1922. The location of the Channahon pavilion is unknown.

LET ME BE YOUR "RAIN-BEAU"

Dearie Mine, the skies are cloudy today,
Dearie Mine the rain is coming they say;
  so blue
Honey don't you sigh, (she) I'm so sad and
  lonely
Honey don't you cry (she) Long for some-one
  only
When rain is falling that's the time I'll come
  to you.
If you will

CHORUS

Let me be your Rain-beau, when the clouds
  roll by,
Let me be your Rain-beau, When the Sun be-
  gins to peep in the Sky.
I'd just love to gather Round you like a cloud,
  and when you're feeling Sky,
I'll let the the sun-shine in-to make you glad.
If you will let me be your rain-beau, When
  the Clouds roll by.   21

As part of the announcement of the "Let Me Be Your Rain-Beau" party, lyrics to a song were included in the invitation. The party took place on June 7, 1922.

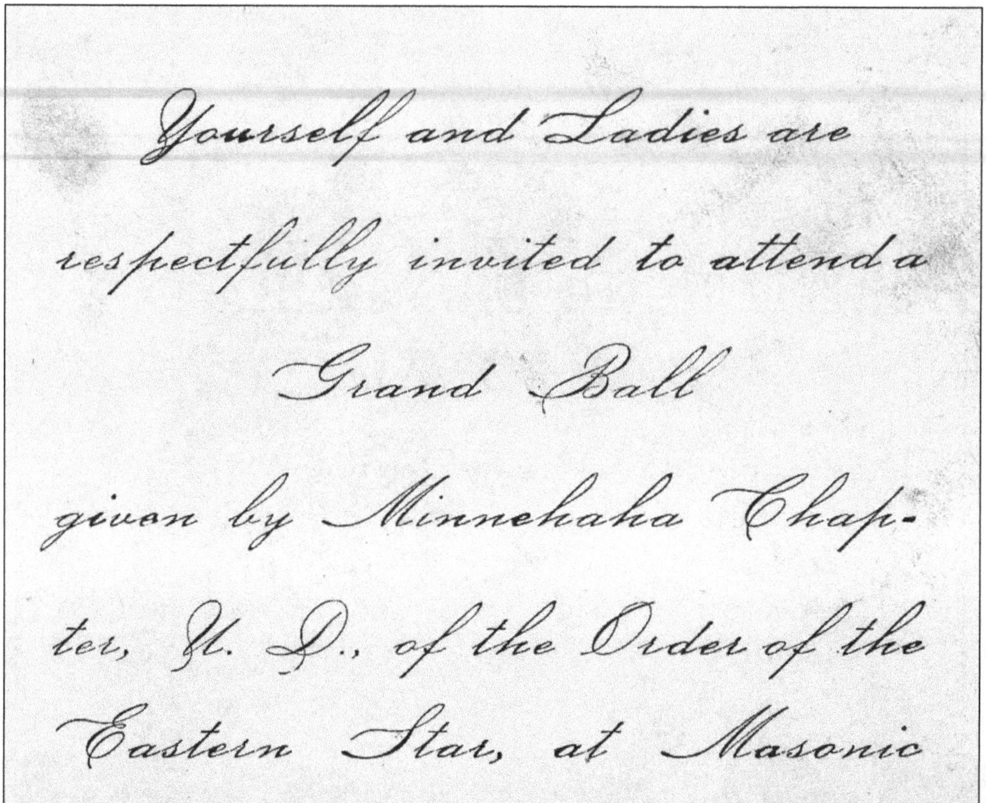

Yourself and Ladies are respectfully invited to attend a Grand Ball given by Minnehaha Chapter, U. D., of the Order of the Eastern Star, at Masonic Hall, Minooka, on Friday Evening, Sept. 7, 1894.

Music by Keene's Orchestra.

Supper furnished by Mrs. Tinder at the Hall.

Dance Ticket, $1.00

Shown here is an invitation to another party at the Masonic lodge. The Grand Ball was hosted by the Minnehaha chapter of the Masonic organization. The event took place on September 7, 1894. The invitation reads "Yourself and Ladies are respectfully invited to attend a Grand Ball given by Minehaha Chapter, U.D., of the Order of the Eastern Star, at Masonic Hall, Minooka, on Friday Evening, Sept. 7, 1894. Music by Keene's Orchestra." The invitation also states that supper will be furnished by Mrs. Tinder. The dance ticket is $1.

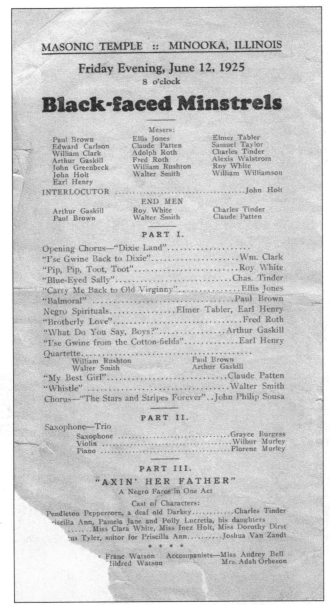

MASONIC TEMPLE :: MINOOKA, ILLINOIS

Friday Evening, June 12, 1925

8 o'clock

Black-faced Minstrels

Messrs:

Paul Brown	Ellis Jones	Elmer Tabler
Edward Carlson	Claude Patten	Samuel Taylor
William Clark	Adolph Roth	Charles Tinder
Arthur Gaskill	Fred Roth	Alexis Walstrom
John Greenbeck	William Rushton	Roy White
John Holt	Walter Smith	William Williamson
Earl Henry		

INTERLOCUTOR ....John Holt

END MEN

| Arthur Gaskill | Roy White | Charles Tinder |
| Paul Brown | Walter Smith | Claude Patten |

PART I.

Opening Chorus—"Dixie Land"...................
"I'se Gwine Back to Dixie".....................Wm. Clark
"Pip, Pip, Toot, Toot".........................Roy White
"Blue-Eyed Sally"..............................Chas. Tinder
"Carry Me Back to Old Virginny"...............Ellis Jones
"Balmoral" ....Paul Brown
Negro Spirituals...............Elmer Tabler, Earl Henry
"Brotherly Love"...............................Fred Roth
"What Do You Say, Boys?"................Arthur Gaskill
"I'se Gwine from the Cotton-fields".............Earl Henry

Quartette.....................................
William Rushton   Paul Brown
Walter Smith   Arthur Gaskill

"My Best Girl"................................Claude Patten
"Whistle" ....Walter Smith
Chorus—"The Stars and Stripes Forever"..John Philip Sousa

PART II.

Saxophone—Trio

Saxophone ....Grayce Burgess
Violin ....Wilbur Murley
Piano ....Florene Murley

PART III.

"AXIN' HER FATHER"

A Negro Farce in One Act

Cast of Characters:

Pendleton Peppercorn, a deaf old Darkey...........Charles Tinder
riscilla Ann, Pamela Jane and Polly Lucretia, his daughters
.......Miss Clara White, Miss Inez Holt, Miss Dorothy Dirst
us Tyler, suitor for Priscilla Ann.........Joshua Van Zandt

* * * *

Franc Watson   Accompanists—Miss Audrey Bell
Iildred Watson   Mrs. Adah Orbeson

A Black-faced Minstrels play was put on in Minooka and included such songs as "I'se Gwine Back to Dixie" and "Carry Me Back to Old Virginny." There are 21 people listed as being involved in the production: Paul Brown, Edward Carlson, William Clark, Arthur Gaskill, John Greenbeck, John Holt, Earl Henry, Ellis Jones, Claude Patten, Adolph Roth, Fred Roth, William Rushton, Walter Smith, Elmer Tabler, Samuel Taylor, Charles Tinder, Alexis Walstrom, Roy White, and William Williamson. In addition, there are three people listed in the saxophone trio: Graycee Burgess, Wilbur Murley, and Florene Murley. Minstrel shows began in the late 1800s in New York City. It was generally a three-part show with people wearing blackface and speaking in what was then understood to be a plantation dialect. Although today these shows are considered offensive, between 1958 and 1978, a show called "The Black and White Minstrel Show" was a huge hit on BBC. It was through minstrel shows that songs such as, "Oh! Susanna" and "Camptown Races" became popular.

121

Yourself and Ladies are cordially invited
to attend a

SOCIAL PARTY

AT

CENTRAL HALL, MINOOKA,

Wednesday Evening, May 2d, 1894.

GRAND MARCH AT 9 P. M.   **Music by Keene's Orchestra.**

Committee of Arrangements:

W. H. KAFFER.   R. E. BRADY.

J. D. DWYER.   F. J. McHUGH.

A social party was held on May 2, 1894. The event was held at Central Hall in Minooka. The history of Central Hall is not known. The top floor of the Minooka Hotel often served as the location for local dances, as did the Masonic lodge. The invitation lists the names W.H. Kaffer, R.E. Brady, J.D. Dwyer, and F.J. McHugh.

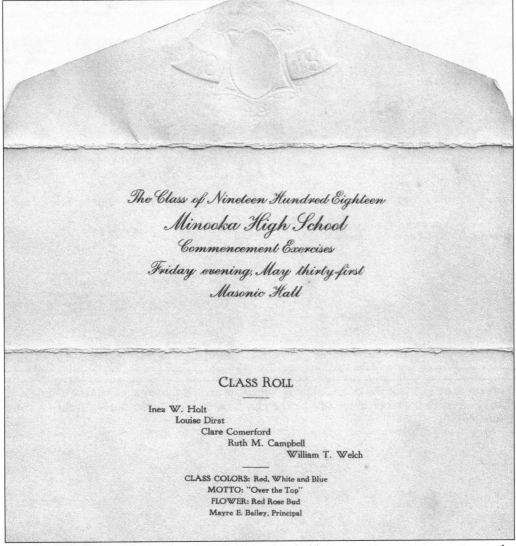

The Class of Nineteen Hundred Eighteen
Minooka High School
Commencement Exercises
Friday evening, May thirty-first
Masonic Hall

CLASS ROLL

Inez W. Holt
Louise Dirst
Clare Comerford
Ruth M. Campbell
William T. Welch

CLASS COLORS: Red, White and Blue
MOTTO: "Over the Top"
FLOWER: Red Rose Bud
Mayre E. Bailey, Principal

In 1918, the Minooka High School graduating class held its commencement exercises at the Masonic lodge. The class graduated only five students. Their names were Inez W. Holt, Louise Dirst, Clare Comerford, Ruth M. Campbell, and William T. Welch. The class colors were red, white, and blue; the motto was "Over the top;" and the class flower was a red rosebud. The principal at the time was Mayre E. Bailey.

PROGRAM

THE STAR COMPANY

Women:	Men:
Lindy Lou	Major Sozo Smith
Araminta Snow	Ebenezer Brown
Chlorinda Dickerson	Snowball Piper *Elmer.*
Eliza Rhee	Pompey Snow
Clover Blossom	Cinnamon Carter
Julianna Snowball	Prof. Artichoke Huggins
Arabella Hastings	Gibraltar White
Bathsheba Blennerhaffett	Celluloid Johnson
Lena Rivers Jordan	Liberty Linkum
Rebecca Dishman	Van Dyke Jefferson
Virginia Johnsing	Gerome Smasher
Clarissa Washington	Gonawanda Hooker *Roy Frachy*
Peggy Black	Tony Bacca Juce
January Sunbeam	Col. Baltimore N. Ohio
Eugenia Jackson	Abraham Linkum Washington

INTERLOCUTOR

Major Sozo Smith—Mr. John Holt

END MEN

Ebenezer Brown, Snowball Piper, Pompey Snow, Cinnamon Carter

Opening Chorus	The Star Company
Lu-li-lu	The Company
Mandy Lee	Araminta Snow
Carve Dat Possum	Snowball Piper
Down in Downy Cotton Town	Ebenezer Brown
Back in Dixie Land	Clover Blossom
Mighty Lak' a Rose	January Sunbeam
Hear Dem Bells	Gibraltar White

PROGRAM

Solid Ground—Pianologue	Gerome Smasher
Buckwheat Cakes	End Men

Assisted by Araminta Snow, Arabella Hastings, Peggy Black and Lena Rivers Jordan.

Celebratin' Day in Tennessee	Peggy Black
Run, Brudder Rabbit, Run!	Cinnamon Carter and Company
Carolina Hills	Rebecca Dishman
My Coal Black Lady	Col. Baltimore N. Ohio
Croon Song	Chlorinda Dickerson
My Own United States	Star Company and Audience

INTERMISSION

Reading—Selected	Madam Clarissa Washington
Pianologue—Selected	Gonawanda Hooker
Piano and Drums—Selected, Bathsheba Blennerhaffett, Snowball Piper	

PART II.

Scene at Railway Station, Coonsville.   Familiar Plantation Songs.

INTERMISSION

A Group of Dixie Songs.

No. 1—Gonawanda Hooker and Snowball Piper.

No. 2—Eliza Rhee, Lena Rivers Jordan and Clover Blossom.

No. 3—Prof. Artichoke Huggins, Abraham Linkum Washington, Celluloid Johnson, Cinnamon Carter and Col. Baltimore N. Ohio.

PART III.

The Old Plantation Ball.

Frances S. Watson, Director.

This is the program for the Star Company, which apparently hosted a play in the community. The contents of the program reveal that the play was set in a railroad station in the southern United States.

Nine

PAST AND PRESENT

This is the front gate to Aux Sable Cemetery, located on Cemetery Road. The site is a garden cemetery and a settler's cemetery. It has been featured on a number of ghost-hunting shows and is rumored to be haunted. Because of this, police watch the cemetery, and the gate is shut at sundown to dissuade trespassers and vandals. (Photograph by Dawn Aulet.)

The Sand Ridge Road Bridge went over the Aux Sable Creek and served as access to the Gleaners Hall. The bridge was dynamited in the 1960s.

The Minooka Grain, Lumber & Supplies Company has been around for 20 years, but the roots of the company extend back to 1908 when it was part of a farmers' cooperative. As farmland began to disappear, the company shifted its focus to the lumber business. (Photograph by Dawn Aulet.)

Visit us at
arcadiapublishing.com

CPSIA information can be obtained
at www.ICGtesting.com
Printed in the USA
LVHW100931300720
661935LV00028B/1019

9 781531 667931